Dear
Peggy,

My lifelong friend
I am truly blessed.
I Love You!

Love,
Deb.

GOOD FRIENDS

Sellers Publishing, Inc.

P. O. Box. 818, Portland, Maine 04104

For ordering information:

(800) 625-3386 toll-free

(207) 772-6814 fax

Visit our Web site: www.rsvp.com • E-mail: rsp@rsvp.com

ISBN 13: 978-1-4162-0524-1

Printed and bound in Canada.

Please note: Every attempt has been made to contact current copyright holders when
appropriate. Any omission is unintentional and the publisher welcomes hearing from any
copyright holders not acknowledged. Omissions will be corrected in subsequent printings.

10 9 8 7 6 5 4 3

GOOD FRIENDS

Are Hard to Find

SELLERS
PUBLISHING

To: _____

From: _____

She is funny, warm, solicitous, caring, kind — everything you want out of a good friend.

— LESLIE HOWLE

It's the friends you can call up at 4 a.m. that matter.

Give me one friend, just one,
who meets the needs of all
my varying moods.

— ESTHER M. CLARK

Promise me you'll always remember: You're braver than you believe, and stronger than you seem, and smarter than you think.

– CHRISTOPHER ROBIN TO POOH, A. A. MILNE

The best mirror is a good friend.

– GEORGE HERBERT

If you find it in your heart to care
for somebody else, you will
have succeeded.

— MAYA ANGELOU

It takes a long time to grow an old friend.

— JOHN LEONARD

When you're looking for a friend, don't look for perfection, just look for friendship.

– IRISH PROVERB

We are designed for love,
not loneliness.

– AUTHOR UNKNOWN

Friendship is a sheltering tree.

– SAMUEL TAYLOR COLERIDGE

A good friend
is cheaper
than therapy.

– AUTHOR UNKNOWN

Life loves to be taken by the lapel and tol

am with you kid. Let's go!'

– MAYA ANGELOU

A good friend is a connection to life — a tie to the past, a road to the future, the key to sanity in a totally insane world.

– LOIS WYSE

Little friends may prove great friends.

— AESOP

Friends are kisses
blown to us by angels.

– AUTHOR UNKNOWN

Are you upset little friend?
Have you been lying awake worrying?
Well, don't worry . . . I'm here.
The flood waters will recede,
the famine will end, the sun will shine
tomorrow, and I will always be here
to take care of you.

– CHARLIE BROWN TO SNOOPY, CHARLES M. SCHULZ

Lots of people want to ride with you in the limo, but what you want is someone who will take the bus with you when the limo breaks down.

— OPRAH WINFREY

To err is dysfunctional,
to forgive co-dependent.

— BERTON AVERRE

Life is partly what we make it, and partly what it is made by the friends we choose.

— TENNESSEE WILLIAMS

A journey is best
measured in friends
rather than miles.

— TIM CAHILL

Things are only impossible
until they're not.

– CAPTAIN JEAN-LUC PICARD,
STAR TREK: THE NEXT GENERATION

One measure of friendship consists not in the number of things friends can discuss, but in the number of things they need no longer mention.

– CLIFTON FADIMAN

Truly great friends are hard
to find, difficult to leave,
and impossible to forget.

– G. RANDOLF

My mother used to say
that there are no strangers,
only friends you haven't met
yet. She's now in a maximum
security twilight home
in Australia.

– DAME EDNA EVERAGE

The only thing to do is to hug one's

friend tight and do one's job.

– EDITH WHARTON

Trust your instincts.
If you have no instincts,
trust your impulses.

– NOËL COWARD

I can only think of one thing greater than being happy and that is to help another to be happy, too.

— JIM THOMSON

*A real friend is someone
who walks in when
the rest of the world
walks out.*

– ITALIAN PROVERB

Don't let anyone tell you that you have to be a certain way. Be unique. Be what you feel.

– MELISSA ETHERIDGE

A loyal friend laughs at your jokes when they're not so good, and sympathizes with your problems when they're not so bad.

– ARNOLD H. GLASGOW

The friend is the one who knows all about you, and still likes you.

– ELBERT HUBBARD

Are we not like two volumes
of one book?

– MARCELINE DESBORDES-VALMORE

The best thing to hold onto
in life is each other.

— AUDREY HEPBURN

Nothing can come
between true friends.

– EURIPEDES

The friend who holds your hand and says the wrong thing is made of dearer stuff than the one who stays away.

— BARBARA KINGSOLVER

To see takes time, like to have a friend takes time.

– GEORGIA O'KEEFFE

Strength lies in differences,
not in similarities.

– STEPHEN COVEY

Shared joys
make a friend.

– FRIEDRICH WILHELM NIETZSCHE

In my friend, I find a second self.

– ISABEL NORTON

There is a voice

inside which

speaks and says:

'This is the real me!'

— WILLIAM JAMES

Happiness can be found,
even in the darkest of times,
if one only remembers to
turn on the light.

– DUMBLEDORE, HARRY POTTER AND THE PRISONER
OF AZKABAN, WARNER BROTHERS, 2004

Best friends listen to
what you don't say.

— TIM MCGRAW

Only your real friends
will tell you when your
face is dirty.

– SICILIAN PROVERB

A friend is someone who lets you ha

otal freedom to be yourself.

– JIM MORRISON

A true friend is someone that knows the song of your soul and sings it back to you when you have forgotten the words.

– AUTHOR UNKNOWN

There is one friend
in the life of each of us
who seems not a separate person,
however dear and beloved,
but an expansion,
an interpretation, of one's self,
the very meaning of one's soul.

– EDITH WHARTON

Sometimes you can't see
yourself clearly until you
see yourself through the
eyes of others.

— ELLEN DEGENERES

No one can be happy without a friend, nor be sure of his friend till he is unhappy.

— THOMAS FULLER

One does not make friends.
One recognizes them.

— GARTH HENRICHS

Friendship
needs
no words...

– DAG HAMMARSKJOLD

Happiness is a
warm puppy.

– CHARLES M. SCHULZ

Friendship is the hardest thing in the world to explain. It's not something you learn in school. But if you haven't learned the meaning of friendship, you really haven't learned anything.

– MUHAMMAD ALI

However rare true love is,
true friendship is rarer.

— FRANÇOIS DE LA ROCHEFOUCAULD